ITALY
A PICTURE BOOK TO REMEMBER HER BY

Designed by
DAVID GIBBON

Produced by
TED SMART

CRESCENT BOOKS
NEW YORK

Italy has always held a powerful attraction for the peoples of Europe. From the barbarian invasions to today's mass tourism, the country has lost none of its magnetism during the millennia of its changing history. Divided for centuries into countless small states, politically weak and therefore the plaything of the European powers, it nevertheless was, and still remains, one of the countries at the centre of Western civilization.

For the traveller in search of sun and sea Italy's climate is one of its main attractions. Down the whole length of the peninsula, however, there is considerable variation. Nevertheless, in the main tourist centres, one can almost always rely on a long, hot summer. Severe winters are normally only found in the Po Valley. In Turin, for example, the average winter temperature is below one degree Celsius. Many areas are at their most pleasant, from the point of view of climate, in autumn and spring.

The beauty of the Italian landscape also contributes to its popularity. In the north the Alps form the frontier with France, Switzerland, Yugoslavia and Austria. Among them are such well-known peaks as the Matterhorn, Gran Paradiso and Monte Rosa, Italy's highest mountain. The Dolomites, with their rugged and sometimes even slightly eerie rock massifs, form part of the eastern Alps. High mountain pastures lead down to the north Italian lakes, and names such as Lago di Como, Lago di Garda and Lago Maggiore inspire thoughts of stretches of blue water with a backdrop of imposing mountains. More than one third of the country is mountainous, and south of the Po Valley the Apennines stretch rather like a backbone down the middle of Italy. Tuscany, with Florence, and Umbria, with Perugia, contain charming scenery, while further south the rocky Mediterranean coast continues through the elegant watering places of Capri and the Campanian coast. Olives, wine and wheat, the main products of the Mediterranean lands, are grown throughout the country, and Italy leads the commercial world as a producer of lemons.

But Italy's most stunning attribute is its vast wealth of art and architecture. The oldest art treasures date from the 5th and 6th centuries BC. In those days southern Italy – the territory of Magna Graecia – was colonised by the Greeks who left behind them superb Doric temples in addition to many other works of art, in Pesto and Agrigento, for example. At about the same time, the western part of central Italy (present day Tuscany) was inhabited by the Etruscans, with their highly-developed culture. Right up to the present day, relics of this culture – gold and silver artefacts, pottery and impressive wall-paintings – have been preserved in burial chambers.

In Rome are to be found masterpieces from every epoch in its history; the most ancient being the ruins of the *Forum Romanum*, once the centre of the old city. In the *quattrocento* (the Italian expression for the 15th century) Romantic and Gothic was followed in Italian art by the Renaissance, the rebirth of the Classical human form and its ideals and standards. The movement began in Florence and produced a profusion of new forms, techniques and knowledge. For example, after studying ancient works of art, Ghiberti created the east door of the Baptistry, the so-called 'Gate to Paradise', and Brunelleschi built his masterpiece, the dome of Florence Cathedral. Sculptors such as Donatello, Luca della Robbia and Verrocchio, painters like Filippo Lippi, Ghirlandajo, Fra Angelico and Botticelli are artists who began the Renaissance. In the 16th century, Rome became the centre of art. The period of the Renaissance was of particular importance for painting, producing artists like Michelangelo, Raphael, Tintoretto, Veronese, Titian and Leonardo da Vinci; all of whose works date from about the same period.

Italy's art treasures are accessible to everyone; they can be visited in palaces, churches, in the country or in the museums of the large towns, and this is for many visitors reason enough to travel to this beautiful country.

The Italians themselves, however, are without any doubt the main attraction. Their lively charm, their delight in colour and form, the beauty of their language and music, their generous natures and their Latin wit make this country a home for all those who are able to maintain their feeling for art in the concrete deserts of today's dull cities.

(Facing page) Lake Garda.

Fare una bella figura (to make a good impression) is a typical Italian aspiration, but it should also be mentioned that, in this case, it is also taken as a mark of common courtesy and consideration for one's neighbour.

If the revolutionary movements of the

A bronze statue of Romulus and Remus (left), the legendary founders of Rome, dating from Etruscan times, may be seen in the city's Capitoline Museum.

The Castel Sant'Angelo (below), whose foundation dates from the time of the Emperor Hadrian.

The Vatican City is the centre of the Roman Catholic Church and at its heart is the Basilica of St Peter (facing page), built over the tomb of the martyred saint, and said to be the most majestic building in the world.

19th century had not driven out the Austrian power, it is probable that Italy would not have leaned towards Freud until much later. Not that this country had been wanting in scholars who indulged in serious and strictly scientific research – we have only to consider Galileo, Galvani, Volta, Pacinotti, Marconi or Fermi – but the sunny image of the Italian way of life is too powerfully reflected in the eyes of a graphic artist for any descent of art into the murky depths of psychoanalysis to be justified.

Art is a gift of grace. Thus Vasari refers to providence in order to find an explanation for Cimabue's birth: 'It was God's will that Giovanni, known as Cimabue, who was later to kindle the first brilliance of Italian painting, was born in the city of Florence in the year 1240'. It is only by drawing on divine providence in this way that the art of a Giotto or a Fra Angelico can be explained. No one else has painted scenes of everday life as Giotto did; he raised them to the heights of mystical poetry: the death of St Francis, the miracle of the *poverello*, the entry of Jesus into Jerusalem. The story goes that Cimabue came upon him one day when he was drawing a sheep on a stone, while tending the cattle in his village. Astonished by his talent, the master took him into his studio and helped him to achieve the fame for which he was so obviously destined.

Whilst Giotto is characterised by a tender naiveté, Fra Angelico is a visionary, wrapped in distant heights. He spent his life in retreat in a monastery and it is said of him that he knelt when he painted the Virgin Mary but could not see for tears when painting Jesus.

Italian painting is toally fulfilling. Simone Martine, Piero della Francesca and Titian were masters of colour; Leonardo, Raphael and Caravaggio draughtsmen of genius; Botticelli and Michelangelo had at their command an inexhaustible imagination.

Nobody, of course, now believes that grace can, in any way, replace lack of effort. Giotto achieved such perfection in his brush control that he could draw an absolutely perfect circle without the aid of a compass or piece of string. Even today there is a vernacular phrase: '*essere*

tondo come l'O di Giotto' (literally: to be as round as Giotto's O; figuratively: a blockhead or ne'er-do-well).

Botticelli spent many an hour with the philosophers at the court of Lorenzo the Magnificent in order to widen his cultural horizons, and it was just this surrender to wisdom which clouded his art when he fell into the clutches of the fanatical monk, Savonarola. Leonardo was a tireless worker and probably the greatest genius in human history. In

Rome is richer in masterpieces, both artistic and architectural, than any other city in the world. Among these are the Colosseum (top left) and the most spectacular of Rome's fountains, the Trevi Fountain (bottom left). Crowds throng the huge area of St Peter's Square (above) while from the pavements outside the cafés (right) the visitor can pause to watch the busy life of the city.

complete secrecy, to avoid being surprised by the authorities, he spent whole nights studying anatomy, using the bodies of those who had been executed. He was a good and generous man, always ready to help another, 'be he rich or poor, if only he shows merit or virtue'. Among his numerous inventions is the design for a submarine, which he naturally did not publish, for 'with it man, naturally wicked, might commit crimes on the seabed by piercing ships' hulls'.

One of the highest mountains in the Alpine range which separates Switzerland and Italy is the Matterhorn (facing page). On its lower slopes is the popular skiing resort of Cervinia-Breuil, with its beautiful surrounding countryside (right).

The 14th-century fortress at Fenis (below) lies in the lovely Valle d'Aosta, a region made up of a series of valleys surrounded by the high peaks of the Matterhorn, Gran Paradiso and Mont Blanc, and renowned for its pleasant and healthy climate.

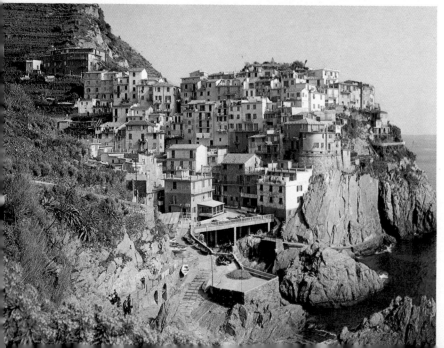

The Italian Riviera, like its French counterpart, is a tourist's paradise. The western section, the Riviera di Ponente, specialises in the production of olive oil and also supplies palms to the Vatican for Holy Week. The beach resort of Diano Marina (facing page) dates back to Roman times and was named after the goddess Diana.

The Riviera di Levante, the eastern section, is much more rugged in character and is rich in picturesque little fishing villages and ports like Camogli (above) and Manarola (left).

It is said of Michelangelo, another titanic worker, that he developed a hump because he had to lie on his back for so long when painting the frescoes in the Sistine Chapel. When, at an already advanced age, he was placed in charge of building operations at St Peter's, he was on horseback on the site practically day and night. On February 14th, 1564, it appears that he suffered a stroke and in the afternoon of the 18th he died.

The energetic Donatello was even known to attack his sculptures, and insult them as if they were figures of flesh and blood. While he was working on his masterpiece *Zuccone*, someone heard him shouting at the figure: 'Will you hurry up and live! A plague upon you!' In actual fact, however, he was such a good-natured and generous man that he hung his money-belt over a beam in his studio so that his friends could help themselves from it if they needed to!

Whereas Classical art renounced expressionistic principles in favour of spiritual refinement, popular art, on the other hand, stresses the dramatic qualities of feeling and gesture. Piero della Francesca's *Virgin with Child* allows us to contemplate her serene beauty surrounded by the mystery of the Incarnation. Popular representations of the Virgin, however, depict simple women showing sweetness or suffering in an inappropriately earthly way. They are mothers like any others, caught up in the destiny of their sons. Yet even in this tender naiveté the feeling of beauty prevails over all passions. St Katharine smiles while the shafts of mystic love pierce her body. Piero della Francesca painted Saint Apollonia with the tongs of her martyrdom in her hand and a smile on her lips. Saint Sebastian, transfixed by arrows, speaks to the angels who are bringing him the crown. And the dead Christ by Marco Zoppe seems to feel the caresses of the angels as they float around him.

The queen of Italy's spiritual life is the *madonna,* just as the mother is sovereign in her family's life. Districts, streets and shops are always under the protection of a madonna. It is to the madonna that altar candles and feasts are offered, and to whom one turns in times of happiness or sorrow. Even if the married man feels like a *pappagallo* in the village square and

Richard the Lionheart, on his way to Syria, took shelter from a stormy sea in Portofino (facing page) on the Riviera di Levante. It has since become the haunt of many artists and writers. The 13th-century castle at Lerici (top), a few kilometres down the coast, is a rare example of Italian medieval military architecture. Vernazza (above) is one of the towns of the Cinqueterre, a region noted for its strong, sweet wine, known to the inhabitants as *schiacchetrà* – the chatterer.

chats up the girls, he keeps his feathers to himself at home in order to win over his jealous and peerless wife.

The miracle of life begins with woman. In 1953 the Holy Virgin in Syracuse burst into tears. Later, tears glistened on the cheeks of all madonnas and, finally, even good Joseph took the side of woman – what fiancé could ever withstand a woman's tears? – and also began to weep in all Italian churches.

It is sometimes difficult to discover where religion ends and superstitious rite begins. Pagan customs have been poetically mingled with Christian liturgy. In many places saints are honoured as protection from the evil eye (the *jettatura*); and in many newspapers fortune-tellers advertise their services with amazing promises: 'Fortune-teller from the East casts the Tarot, foretells the future and breaks the curse of the *jettatura*'.

Pagan customs have survived in carnival festivities. In Verona the *Bacchanale del Gnocco* is celebrated every year. In Venice, San Remo and Viareggio the carnival is held with processions and dancing, but with rather less Dionysian abandon.

Towards the end of the last century the people of Sardinia used to gather on the squares, where condemned prisoners were usually executed, in order to carry out nightly rites in memory of those who had been beheaded. In Venetia, where it is believed that the mother of Saint Peter went to eternal damnation because of

The Italian Lake District lies at the foot of the Alps and the idyllic beauty of this combination of mountains and water has attracted visitors from all over the world. The varied scenery of Lake Maggiore (facing page) has made it particularly popular. In fine weather the waters appear green in the north and brilliant blue in the south.

The largest of the lakes is Lake Garda (top left). It is 52 kilometres long and a depth of 346 metres has been recorded. The lake at Molveno (bottom left) feeds one of the most important hydro-electric schemes in Europe. The village provides a base for mountain climbers attempting the peaks of the Brenta Massif.

her avarice (they still say today: *l'e àvaro como sò mama de San Piero* – he is as stingy as Saint Peter's mother), incantations are made on the 29th June to release the poor old woman from Hell and enable her to visit her son in Heaven. In Cagliari they still celebrate the 'Ides of May' with magnificent processions in honour of the madonna; and in Gagliano the people offer fruit and eggs to the 'Black Madonna'.

The most famous of all matriarchal festivals, however, takes place in Naples when the *madonna di piedigrotta* processes through the streets of the city accompanied by a crowd using every kind of instrument to produce the most raucous of sounds.

Midsummer night is still filled with miracles. Friends meet the previous evening in Rome to eat a delicious snail dish together. Whoever partakes is protected from quarrelling, for the horns of snails are the symbol of brawling and wrangling. During the night of the 24th June, however, prodigies prevail. Those curious to see witches wait at crossroads, their chins propped on a hayfork. Prudent folk, on the other hand, who wish to avoid the evil visitors, bar their front doors by fixing a broom across them – for before they can enter a house, the daughters of Satan have to count every single bristle in the broom.

The devil is a tiresome character given to coarse jokes, but he sometimes reveals a not entirely wicked side. According to tradition, he built the Arena at Verona in addition to several other imposing structures. A few lesser 'devils' are more like dwarves, like the *massariol* who eats honey and plays the fiddle on winter nights. In the church of Santa Caterina in Treviso the demon-king is represented disguised as a woman. Next to the real devils, there are, as there are everywhere, more human 'devils'. The most famous among these was the Venetian Alvise Veneto, who was condemned to wander without rest through the city with devil's horns on his head as a punishment for forcing his wife into prostitution...but mainly because he diligently recorded his income from this 'trade' in a book!

New Year's Eve is the festival of renewal. Romans make it known that they support this welcome occasion by throwing every possible old or broken object out of the window for the rag-and-bone man to remove: crockery, bottles,

The countryside above Lake Garda (top left) has a peace and beauty matching that of the lake itself.

The praises of Lake Como have been sung by Pliny, Virgil and Shelley, and Lezzeno (right) is one of the villages that border its shores.

The baroque church of Sacre Monte (bottom left) lies above Lake Varese and is the scene of an important pilgrimage to the Virgin. It stands at an altitude of 880 metres and has outstanding views over the surrounding lakes.

broken chairs and possibly an out-of-tune piano, which may fall on the head of a hapless night reveller who would really like to see in the first day of the New Year. In Vittorio Veneto large piles of wood are set on fire on the surrounding hills in honour of the Three Kings. When the

flames go out, another fire must quickly be lit to avoid future calamities.

Yet it is not only religious festivals which provide an opportunity for giving full rein to joy and imagination. Historical anniversaries also have their magic moments. In one festival Rovigo recalls

---

Milan is the economic capital of Ìtaly; an industrial, commercial and banking centre which every year plays host to an important International Trade Fair.

Built of white marble, Milan Cathedral (left) is at the heart of the city. Although it was started in 1386 the facade was only finished in 1809, by order of Napoleon, and it was not finally completed until 1897.

In the church of Sant'Ambrogio is a fine, 9th-century altar frontal (above). It is made of gold and silver plates sculpted in relief, studded with gems and inlaid with enamel, and represents scenes from the life of Christ and of Saint Ambrose.

the popular uprising which brought to an end the unbridled despotism of the Margrave of Montferrato. In Trentino, too, a medieval tyrant is burnt in effigy. On May 15th Gubbio commemorates the town's victory over eleven hostile towns with the *festa dei ceri* (festival of candles). Also of historical origin is the Venetian festival of the *sensa* (Ascension) which solemnises the ritual marriage of the Doge with the sea, just as it was celebrated in the Renaissance. On board the gilded *bucintoro* the Doge sailed across the lagoon to the island of Saint Elena where he met the patriarch. Then, on the open sea, he threw his ring into the water, while he pronounced the following ritual formula: '*Ti sposiamo, o mare, in segno de vero e perpetuo dominio*' (we marry you, O sea, to symbolise true and perpetual dominion).

The most impressive of the historical festivals is the *palio*, which takes place each year in Siena during the months of July and August. In the incomparably beautiful Piazza del Campo representatives of the *contrade*, the different districts of the town of Siena, take part in

a fiercely-contested horse race. In the festive atmosphere the riders appear in 15th-century clothes; entering the contest under the banners of the different districts.

Italian cafés have a long artistic tradition. Wagner used to write in the *Lavenna* in Venice. Papini and his friends met in the Florentine *Guibbe rosse*. Pea and Puccini liked to relax in the *Margheritta* in Viareggio. In Rome D'Annunzio went to the *Faraglia,* and Mendelssohn often went to the long-established *Greco*. Cafés often served as meeting places for secret masonic lodges or for revolution-

Set amid rolling countryside, Lake Misurina (below) was used as the racing ice rink for the 1956 Winter Olympics and is a popular tourist spot.

The Dolomites (remaining pictures) lie to the north-east of the country. They are formed of limestone rock, their pink colouring varying dramatically with the changing light.

(Overleaf): the famous skiing resort of Cortina d'Ampezzo.

Venice, rising from the sea like Venus, is one of the most beautiful cities in the world. The Grand Canal (top right, bottom right and overleaf) winds through the city, with famous palaces and churches lining its banks.

St Mark's Square, with the Campanile and the Doge's Palace, is shown (above), and (left) is part of the facade of St Mark's, with the Doge's Palace, the twin columns and the lagoon beyond.

aries. *Florian,* a famed Venetian café, saw the start of the revolt against Austrian hegemony. But if cafe's are the centre of discussion, or even revolution, the kitchen always remains the refuge of classical, conservative continuity. So it is that the inhabitants of Bologna, the most prominent cooks in the country, are revolutionary in their ideas but conservative at table. It is no accident that pasta products, which express family unity, are the Italian national dish. It is round the daily plateful of pasta that the bonds are forged between the generations. In some areas of Basilicata only macaroni is cooked during the period of mourning following the death of the head of a family.

A country which loves art must inevitably afford its cuisine a privileged position. Just as a declaration of love is made with the help of an Aretino sonnet, so do the Venetians cook cod (*baccalà*) from a recipe which contains twenty-six verses. The most famous of all Italian chefs was the composer Rossini, who also rose to fame by means of a few dishes he invented himself. He was so fat that Gautier's comment on his corpulence was that 'he last saw his feet twenty years ago'. One music critic expressed himself in even more caustic terms, saying that 'in Rossini's orchestra unpleasant background noises could be heard constantly, as if from stewpans and saucepans'. Casanova, too, was a noted gourmet. He particularly liked to 'swallow oysters from his lovers' lips'. One of his favourite dishes was macaroni filled, by means of a forcing bag, with chicken liver purée.

In Italy, pasta and pizza occupy the place which bread and potatoes have in other lands. Napoleon apparently liked *grissini* so much that he always expressed a craving for 'Turin sticks'.

Incomparable Venice: traditional gondolas (left), now taking second place to motor boats as the chief means of transport; St Mark's Square (top right), a popular meeting-place, not least with the pigeons, which come down in flocks to be fed, and the Rialto Bridge (bottom right), designed to allow an armed galley to pass underneath.

Like Raphael's painting, Italian cookery is ample and entirely the product of a radiant Mediterranean culture. Its brilliant colours are typical – tomato red, paprika green and lemon yellow – their contrasts gently softened by aromatic olive oil.

As in painting, so in the kitchen. Italians succeed in cooking a wide selection of dishes with simple trimmings; a selection which is further enriched from region to region by various skilful additions. In Venetia food is chiefly served on a base of *fruits de mer* (cuttlefish, crab, *masanette*) and rice. Among meat dishes *fegato alla veneziana* (grilled calf's liver with onions) – with which Polenta is eaten – wins the highest praise. Marzipan, *torta de mandorle* (almond flan) or delicious ice cream is recommended for dessert.

The inhabitants of the Po Valley are renowned for their rice dishes. The regional dish is simply *risotto alla milanese* whose golden grains gleam like a landscape in the evening sun. The rice, which is prepared in gravy, is cooked with butter, saffron, chicken liver, beef marrow and cheese. Lombardy is the district for cheeses and they are produced there in choice abundance, from *bel paese* or *stracchino* to the *gorgonzola* of universal renown. A *cotoletta milanese* is cooked with a little grated cheese, egg and breadcrumbs. For dessert there is *panettone*, also from Milan, cakes made of very fine flour, butter, eggs, sultanas and preserved fruits.

The addition of the words *alla genovese* always denotes food to which a refined mélange of wild herbs adds a special zest. Alpine basil, nuts and grated cheese form the basis of *pesto*, a sauce which is served with pasta. *Il tocco* is a gravy with the added fragrances of tomatoes, celery, onions and mushrooms. More substantial is the third of the great Genoese sauces, the *agliata*; a mixture containing garlic, crusts of bread and vinegar.

Thick meat sauces *alla bolognese* set the fashion in the Emelia Romagna. The best sausages are produced in Bologna: *mortadella*, *salami*, pig's trotters (*zampone*). To this tasty menu Parma contributes its mature cheeses – which always improve with age – and its world-famous ham.

Tuscan cookery is characterised by its elegant simplicity, with dishes such as Florentine cutlet, roast chicken *all'aretina* or artichoke omelette. But even those who love baroque table delights find satisfaction with luscious sweet-and-sour (*agrodolce*) hare in a sauce whose main ingredients are chocolate, vinegar, sultanas and pine kernels!

In Ancona, substantial fish casseroles are a speciality. The fish is caught in the waters of the Adriatic, and the height of enjoyment, without any doubt at all, is their fish soup (*brodetto*).

Umbria is better known for its Franciscan moderation and thrift than its cuisine. Nevertheless, it is the home of juicy sucking pig, which is roasted and seasoned with rosemary, garlic and pepper. Black truffles are sold throughout Europe under the name of 'Truffles from Périgord'. These grow in the woods round Spoleto and Norcia and were once widely renowned as aphrodisiacs.

As is well-known, all roads lead to Rome, and that being so we find an unsurpassable synthesis of Italian cuisine in the capital. To prepare fish in breadcrumbs *a la romana*, olive oil is used, but Romans are also great lovers of lard (*estrutto*), which is used for roasting other dishes. For example, *saltimbocca* –

Verona was the home of the Montagues and the Capulets, immortalised in Shakespeare's play *Romeo and Juliet*. The balcony (top left) is of the 13th-century house in the Via Capello in which Juliet is said to have lived. The entrance porch of the church of San Zeno (bottom left), also in Verona, is remarkable for the 11th to 12th-century doors encased in bronze plates depicting scenes from the Old and New Testaments.

Fifty kilometres down the coast from Ravenna is the Republic of San Marino. It is one of the smallest and most ancient states in the world, has its own coinage, and an army of 120 soldiers. Two notable buildings are the Government House (top right) and the Fortress (bottom right).

(Overleaf): the Cathedral, Baptistry and Leaning Tower of Pisa.

It is easy to think of Florence (above) as an enormous museum, so great is its heritage of masterpieces of art and architecture.

Faced with green, white and red marble, the Cathedral of Santa Maria del Fiore (facing page) was begun in 1296. The magnificent dome took fourteen years to build and the stained glass windows were made following cartoons by Castagno, Ghiberti, Donatello and Uccello. Beside the cathedral stands the Campanile designed by Giotto.

The home of Dante, another of Florence's famous sons, is shown (bottom right).

veal cut into pieces with the addition of ham and, as a refinement, a few drops of Marsala – is fried in lard. *Battuto* is a mixture of bacon, garlic, parsley and celery.

Naples is the capital of pasta dishes, of *pizza*, fish and tomato. Therefore, it comes as no surprise to learn that Neapolitans claim to have discovered the art of cooking. There is also no lack of excellent sausages; among them the smoked sausage from Secondigliano and the small Neapolitan sausages. Close to these in renown, and deservedly so, is Neapolitan puff pastry and the

On either side of Florence's Ponte Vecchio (facing page) are gold- and silversmiths' shops that date back to the 16th century.

The facade of the Basilica of San Miniato del Monte (left), near Florence, and (below) the floodlit tower of the Palazzo della Signoria, shining over the city of Florence at night.

almost endless variety of ice cream.

The further south we go, towards Calabria and Sicily, the simpler and more highly spiced the food becomes. The liberal use of pepper characterises pasta in Calabria. From the Basilicata come noteworthy cheeses: piquant *cacciocavallo*, sarp *provolone*, fat *anteche* and the outstanding *ricotta*, a cheese made from ewe's milk. The South is the home of fruits which thrive in a hot climate: lemons, oranges, grapes, figs...and we should not forget the olives which probably contributed to the fact that the first homesick settlers in the Greek colonies felt attracted to this country.

The motto of Siena, *Cor magis tibi Sena pandit*, translates as 'Siena opens its heart to you' – and it is, indeed, a warm and welcoming place. The famous *Palio* horse race takes place twice a year in the city's square (above).

The striking cathedral (top right), with its restored facade of multi-coloured marble, was begun in 1065 and contains works by Bernini, Raphael and Donatello.

A partial view (bottom right) of one of the rooms in the Palazzo Pubblico.

Outside Siena is the old fortress of Monteriggioni (bottom left).

The island of Elba (these pages) lies 18 kilometres off the west coast of Italy and is best-known as the temporary home of Napoleon after his abdication in 1814. Both the houses he occupied are open to the public and contain collections of his furniture, books and other mementoes. Vines and olives grow in profusion in the island's warm climate and in recent years many holiday-makers have enjoyed its rocky beaches, potent white wine and peaceful atmosphere.

Where wine is concerned, Italy is a blessed land. Every single region produces white and red wines which command high prices in the markets of the world: from Venetia comes red *Valpolicella* with a taste reminiscent of bitter almonds; from Trentino the finest sparkling wines – the patriarchal *Terlano* becomes cheerier the older it is. Piedmont is the home of rich, heavy wines. *Barbera* goes supremely well with game, and *Barolo* is best drunk with roast meat. Umbria can be proud of its clear, pure, transparent wines, like the wine from Orvieto. In the Rome region we find the dry *Frascati* or *Montefiascone*. In Naples the vines get sustenance from the volcanic soil of Vesuvius: *Lacrimae Christi, Falernum, Capri, Ischia...* Neapolitan grape juice can point to a long and noble history. Even Trajan praised the wines from Salerno, and he drank them after they had been in the cellar for two hundred years! From Sicily it is *Marsala*, the sweet wines from Syracuse and *Malvasia* from Lipari which deserve mention.

But there is one more wine which should not be forgotten – the international wine, but at the same time the most intrinsically Italian wine – *Chianti* from Tuscany, famous for over six hundred years. In straw-clad bottles it spends its life in semidarkness and is always better with age.

'All of us are pilgrims to Italy', wrote Goethe. There have been few artists, from Cervantes to Byron, from Mateo Alemán to Ibsen, from George Sand to Hemingway, who have resisted the call of Italy.

Cervantes praises 'the beauty of Naples, the leisureliness of Palermo, the abundance of Milan, the revelling in Lombardy, the superb inn cuisine', and while allowing shafts of his critical judgement of gastronomical matters to shine through – which he was to bring to fruition later in his masterpieces – he praises 'the mildness of Trevianer wine, the strength of Montefiascone, the sharpness of Asperiner, the nobility of the two Greek wines, Candía and Soma, the quantity of wine from the five vineyards, the sweetness and peaceable nature of Signora Vernaccia, the peasant quality of Centola in whose company

Romanesco in its meanness did not dare show itself'.

Cervantes, also a courteous and observant traveller, finds words of praise for every town in Italy. He remembers the hospitality of Lucca, the charm of Florence's river, and he raises Rome to the rank of a 'queen among cities and ruler of the world'. In his book *El Licenciado Vidriera* he bestows upon the capital an endless garland of dithyrambs: '...He visited its temples, admired its relics and looked with astonishment at its vastness. And just as one can measure a lion's strength and ferocity by its claws, so he became aware of Rome's greatness when he stood before its broken marble, its statuary, whether damaged or whole, its ruined arches and wrecked baths, its magnificent colonnades and gigantic amphitheatres, the famous, holy river whose banks are still filled with water and which beautifies them with the countless relics of the saints who found their graves within it, and with its bridges which seem to watch each other. Also when he was in its streets, which are supreme among all other streets in the world by their names: Via Appia, Via Flamina, Via Julia, and whatever other names they bear. He was just as impressed by the spread of its hills: Celio, Quirinale, Vatican, and four others whose names bear witness to the splendour and majesty of Rome. He was

The town of Assisi (facing page) is still enclosed by ramparts and is little changed since the Middle Ages. It was, of course, the home of St Francis, the son of a rich merchant, and an aggressive and ambitious youth until his conversion. He founded the Franciscan Order of Mendicant Friars, wrote poems and preached on the beauties of nature and love of animals, winning many converts. The basilica (top right) containing his tomb was designed by his friend and follower Brother Elias, and is decorated throughout with frescoes, among them 28 depicting the life of Saint Francis, which have been attributed to Giotto. (Bottom right): a pageant in Ascoli Piceno featuring a knights' tournament.

The barely-slumbering, ominously-smouldering bulk of Mount Etna (above), the largest active volcano in Europe.
The churches of St Dominic (top right) and St Peter (bottom right) are situated in the Umbrian capital of Perugia, a quiet, peaceful town overlooking the historic River Tiber.

probably well aware too of the might of the College of Cardinals, the majesty of the Holy Father, and the thronging multitudes of nations and men. He discovered everything, he was confident and able to cope with their vast numbers. After he had followed the route of the seven churches and made his confession to a priest and kissed His Holiness's foot, he decided to travel on to Naples, having amassed a host of prayers and bills; but as the weather was unsettled, foul and dangerous for anyone leaving or entering Rome, he went by sea to Naples...'

Years later the picture of Rome was still before Don Quixote's author's eyes when he seranaded the city with these lines: 'O great and mighty, most holy, venerable city of Rome! I bow before you, a pious, humble, recent pilgrim, amazed by so much beauty. However lofty the traveller's idea of you may be, it pales before the sight that you present, which is even mightier than your fame. The traveller came to behold you, to admire you, tenderly disposed and barefooted...'

For travellers in the last century Italy finished at Rome, or at the very furthest in Naples. Yet in the same way that the world is richer towards the north and more beautiful towards the south, tourists have discovered the untouched beaches of Sicily and Sardinia, the fishing villages of Calabria and the bright bay of the Mare Piccolo. *Lungomare,* the marine promenade at Reggio, was considered even by D'Annunzio to be 'the most beautiful kilometre in Italy'. Even the last Mediterranean seals (*Manacus albiventer*) did what tourists now do; they took refuge in the Sardinian sea-caves.

Not only do all roads meet at Rome, but also all cultural currents in the European continent. The city owes a good deal of its beauty to the conciliatory power which can unite in a single whole the horizontal lines of the pagan temple with the airy dome of Christendom. Stendhal found appropriate words for this fruitful, aesthetic paradox: 'Had sacerdotal Rome not been built at the expense of ancient Rome, we would today have considerably more Roman buildings. But at the same time Christianity would

not have made such a profound bond with beauty.'

There are also roads, of course, which do not lead to Rome but wind almost unnoticed through the most distant corners of Italy. The earliest travellers in the 18th century, such as Horace Walpole or Winckelmann, concentrated on evidence of antiquity. Italy finished for them with the Juno Ludovisi or the Laocoon. But in the Romantic age a new way of travelling was discovered, more spontaneous and more in tune with the Italian temperament. With these people the extravagant youth of the English Romantic movement came to the Apennine peninsula with the three princes of poetry: Byron, Shelley and Keats. The last two were to die in Italy – the one falling foul of stormy weather, the other of fever. Meanwhile, Byron swam across the Lido from Venice, took part in the Carbonari plot in the café Florian or indulged in intense altercations with his lady-loves. Yet life was easy for that young gentleman, who admitted that he 'had the same income as the President of the United States, the British Foreign Minister or the French Ambassador in Vienna'.

Perhaps no other traveller in Italy, before or after him, enjoyed more popularity than Byron. He walked in Pisa accompanied by a countess, eight dogs, three monkeys, five cats, an eagle, a parrot and a falcon. He was as reckless as any real Venetian, such as Marco Polo or Casanova. When he returned from the East, Marco Polo told unbelievable stories, to anyone who wished to hear, about that unknown part of the earth: distances of millions of kilometres, millions of pearls, millions of workers occupied building the imperial palaces

The Isle of Ischia lies in the Bay of Naples and is rapidly becoming as popular as its near neighbour, Capri. The Castle of Ischia (top left and facing page) is built on a rocky islet at the end of a man-made bridge. Though known as the *Castello* it comprises several churches and other buildings as well as the ruins of a 15th-century castle.
(Bottom left): a view of Positano in the Bay of Naples.

The tourist making a first visit to Naples (facing page) is recommended to approach by sea. This will allow the opportunity to absorb the magnificent vista of castles, hills, and ancient and modern buildings, surrounded by blue sea and sky and all dominated by the brooding presence of Vesuvius. Another attraction is the people. Almost a nation in their own right, the Neapolitans are renowned for their gaiety and vitality, their love of song, sense of humour and spontaneity. The Neapolitan fondness for music is reflected in the popularity of the San Carlo Theatre (above) which in Italy ranks second only in importance to La Scala, Milan.

Capri is one of the favourite spots of the international jet set and has, throughout the centuries, provided a home for many famous people, from the Emperor Tiberius to Gracie Fields. The Swedish writer, Axel Munthe, wrote of the atmosphere of the island in his book *The Story of San Michele*, and from the piazza of his home, the Villa San Michele, there are magnificent views (above) of the surrounding countryside.
Capri's Marina Piccola (facing page) provides the best bathing on the island. In the distance, just off the coast, is the Faraglioni Rock.
(Overleaf): the Gladiators' Barracks and part of the Great Theatre of Pompeii, the Roman town destroyed by the eruption of Vesuvius nearly two thousand years ago.

Sardinia, the second largest island in the Mediterranean, is changing rapidly with the increase in tourism and the growth of industry, but it is still an island of contrasts. Shepherds dressed in goatskins still look after their flocks in the valleys while holiday-makers in bikinis sun themselves on the beaches; ancient streets lead to modern buildings, and in the harbours fishing boats rub shoulders with elegant, ocean-going yachts. The island's picturesque capital, Cagliari, founded by the Phoenicians, has become an important tourist centre. Monuments from Roman times, and evidence of the Spanish presence, are still to found on Sardinia.

and roads... The Venetians, familiar with his flights of imagination, called him *'il millione'* for they never had much confidence in the veracity of Marco Polo's long-winded stories.

Venice was also where George Sand lived with Alfred de Musset, the man who wanted to be buried under a weeping willow. His friends planted a willow tree on his grave in Paris, but it would never grow properly, just as his love for the adventurous George Sand was never quite reciprocated, and she soon left her romantic poet for a Venetian doctor called Pagello. But because a Venetian of real worth never leaves a rival in command of the field, there were dreadful scenes in the Corte Minelli house. One such battle left the handsome Pagello in a very sorry state, given such a hiding that Sand, shocked, wrote in her diary: 'I felt as if I was carrying out a surgical operation on thirty dismembered cats'.

Whatever should one say about Naples, the capital of rioting, the queen of light, sea and noise? But let us not be too hasty. Scandal in Naples is like the foyer in a theatre, like the rough outline of a statue. And as far as noise is concerned ...'It is enough to stop for a moment' writes Guido Piovene 'and listen to the clamour of Naples, the shouting from the water or the cries of the cherry sellers. I have often heard the cries modulate from one key to another in the popular quarters of Naples; just like the sounds of the East, and perhaps that is the true Neapolitan music.'

Let us go further southwards, to Syracuse and Palermo. Here history has changed into fields of wheat, into golden dust, browned by the sun, a harsh land where, in a strange way, love and revenge take root together. 'I'll kill you if I can' goes a terrible Sicilian proverb, and this is strictly followed in cases of *vendetta,* 'but if I die, I'll forgive you'.

In the *mezzogiorno* Arabia or Paradise begins: extensive beaches with white sand, orange trees, palms, lemon trees and beetling crags over the blue sea. Danger begins here too: yesterday the Mafia, today oil.

Finally, Sardinia; island of honey and fishing, flaky pastry *(carta di musica)* and prehistoric fortifications. Even meat

here is roasted in a stone-lined pit *(carriargu)*, exactly as the shepherds of antiquity cooked it.

We have the construction of the *autostrade* to thank for the fact that it is child's play to cover vast distances in Italy. Sometimes, because of the speed involved, travelling becomes a game which makes one dizzy. Whereas the *'serenissima'* crosses the peninsula horizontally from Turin to Venice, the traveller reaches the deep south of the country on the eight hundred-kilometre-long *'Autostrada del Sole'*.

But what really matters is improvisation, instinct and delight in various forms: the Alpine lakes, or the delights of dreaming; Naples, or the delights of living; Florence, or visual delights.

The first travellers to go to Italy went with the desire to trade. When the Carthaginian Hanno set out to sail round the African coasts, his chief aim was to establish new markets for Punic trade. The Cretans took wine and olive oil to Egypt and in exchange brought back ivory and gold from Africa. The enclosed and easily navigable Mediterranean favoured this exchange of goods. 'Our city's renown attracts businessmen from all over the world', said the Athenian Pericles. And even Plato, who, as a Utopian and doctrinaire thinker, was not exactly a supporter of the commercial way of life, acknowledged that the exchange of goods is the best way of balancing the lack of equilibrium bestowed by nature. The Romans built their empire on the basis of a solid and sure trade network, and this is how great centres of commerce like Rome, Alexandria, Tarragona and Cadiz grew up in the Mediterranean world. The history of

The coast from Sorrento to Salerno – the Costa Amalfitina – contains some of the most fashionable holiday resorts in Italy. The coast road is said to be one of the most beautiful in the world and the scenery is certainly spectacular.
Atrani (facing page and top left) is a fishing village at the mouth of the dramatically-named Dragon Valley.
(Bottom left) is shown another, smaller, fishing village near Amalfi.

Positano (facing page, top) is one of the most important resorts on the Costa Amalfitina. It was once a fishing village and the old town still remains intact (above).

The cathedral at Amalfi (facing page, bottom) dates back to the 11th century, a time when Amalfi was one of the great cities of Italy. A succession of tidal waves which destroyed ships in the harbour and washed away parts of the town resulted in a decline in prosperity.

trade was given an enormous boost in the cities of the Italian Renaissance, favoured by scientific discoveries such as the compass, by means of which mariners now sailed the world oceans from Amalfi or Genoa. In Florence, in the 15th century, the Medicis founded the most important commercial enterprises of all time. Not much later the Genoese opened their bank of the 'Casa di San Giorgio', while the Venetians started the 'Banca de Rialto'. Buying and selling are classical methods of discovering a country, especially in the Mediterranean region. And there is much greater importance than is usually acknowledged in the marketing of souvenirs, sometimes cheaply made for the sake of profit. Goethe's love of Italy, for example, started with a souvenir from his youth; it was a miniature gondola which his father had brought back from Venice, a souvenir which the writer sentimentally cherished in his house in Frankfurt.

Scholars usually rack their brains attempting to discover, in the depths of history, the driving force which led to progress or cultural development. But things are sometimes very much simpler than they appear. Henry VIII's lusts or Napoleon's haemorrhoids played just as important a part in the breakaway of the Anglican Church or the defeat at Waterloo as the theologians or politicians with their revolutionary ideas. The Golden Age of German Classicism is to a great extent founded on one small souvenir, the miniature gondola, which old councillor Goethe kept so lovingly from his youth.

Shopping has its own importance and Italy certainly offers the traveller such a wide choice of goods that it becomes a pleasure. The Italians offer not only industrial products of excellent quality, they also keep alive the old traditions of skilled craftsmanship. Who could resist the allure of fine lace in Burano or Bosa and of embroidery in Florence? The best Italian cloth excels through its print and dyeing. Yet the most archaic arts, such as pottery, have also managed to retain their well-earned reputation. Magnificent ceramics are fired in the kilns of Faenza. It is in its historical reputation that one finds the explanation

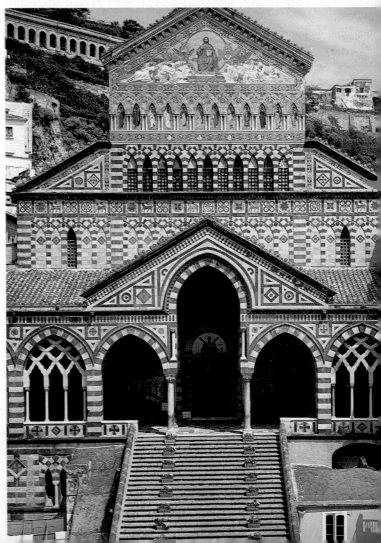

of the fact that porcelain in France is called *'faïence'*. Works in porcelain from Capodimonte and enamelled ceramics from Albisola are also renowned for their exquisite beauty.

Every Italian region or town has its own craft speciality: corals come from Campania or Sicily, pewterware from Brescia, copper from Naples, mosaics from Ravena, glass from Milan, wrought iron from Bologna, woodcarving from the Alpine valleys, wood-inlay work from Sicily and Sardinia, baskets from Castelsardo...

Yet skilled craft, like everything the Italians do, is always on the threshold of becoming pure art. This is the case, for example, with the glass products of Murano. For centuries the craftsmen in this little island in the Venetian lagoon have maintained the strictest secrecy over their manufacturing methods. Glass-blowers even enjoyed certain social privileges. A patrician could marry the daughter of a Murano glass-blower without the children from the marriage losing their noble rights. The most notable piece of work produced by the Murano factories is exhibited in their Glasswork Museum; it is a lamp, designed in 1864 by Angelo Serena, weighing over 300 kilograms.

Is the label 'skilled craft' sufficient for violin making in Cremona? From this wonderful town, the birthplace of Monteverdi, come the best violin-makers of all time: the families of Stradivarius, Guarnerius and Amati. The making of a violin demands just as keen an ear as the orchestration of a symphony. One millimetre too little or too much in the thickness of the belly or a mistake in the composition of the lacquer can ruin even the best instrument. Because of their purity of tone the violins from the Cremona school fetch auction prices as high as does a painting by Sebastiano del Piombo. Amati particularly emphasised

Because of its triangular shape, the Ancient Greeks called Sicily *Trinacria*. The Temple of the Dioscuri – the Heavenly Twins – (right) is in the Valley of Temples, just outside the town of Agricento. Until recently these temples – there are five – were thought to have been ruined by one of the many earthquakes that have punctuated Sicily's history; it now seems more likely, however, that they were destroyed by the early Christians in their campaigns against pagan gods.

Messina (facing page, top) is a busy trading centre with a particularly well-sheltered habour. The cathedral, as well as most of the town, was destroyed in the earthquake of 1908 but has now been almost completely rebuilt.

Palermo is the capital of the island and its chief port. The catheral (facing page, bottom) was founded in the 12th century.

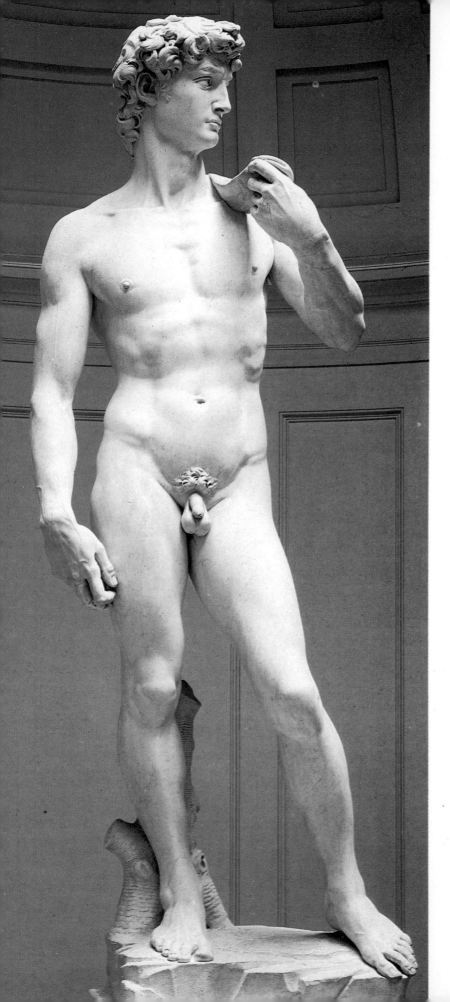

a sweet tone; Stradivarius succeeded in giving his instruments independent sonority within the total orchestral milieu. It is said that the master, Antonio Stradivarius, made more than two thousand stringed instruments during his life. Yet probably the most impressive personality among all the Cremona violin-makers was Guarneri del Gesù, whose instruments Paganini chose for his concerts. In so doing he must certainly have appreciated the gripping pathos of their low notes and the nervous brilliance of their high ones. The famous *cannone* belonging to the Master is preserved in Genoa.

Just as violins continue to be made today in Cremona, accordions are manufactured in Ancona and Stradella, and the mechanical pianos from Casale are also held in high esteem.

The history of tourism begins with trade, it is true, but music makes travelling so much more enjoyable...

Italy has given the world some of the greatest artists of all time. Michelangelo's famous 'David' is shown (left); 'The Adoration of the Magi' by Leonardo da Vinci (facing page, top) and the 'Paradise Gate' in the Baptistry at Florence, by Ghiberti, (facing page, bottom).
(Overleaf): picturesque houses at the water's edge in Sorrento.

CLB 1209
© 1986 Illustrations and text: Colour Library Books Ltd.,
   Guildford, Surrey, England.
Text filmsetting by Acesetters Ltd., Richmond, Surrey, England.
All rights reserved.
1986 edition published by Crescent Books, distributed by Crown Publishers, Inc.
Printed in Spain.
ISBN 0 517 250160
h g f e d c b a

Dep.Leg. B-42.668-85